More Titles Available by John Golden
Roaming Lions Press

A Tear From A Glass Eye (2010)
Sons of the Silent Age (2010)
The Dying Tree (2010)

A Tear
From A
Glass Eye

John Golden

Roaming Lions Press 2010

A Tear From A Glass Eye. Copyright © 2010 by John Golden. All Rights Reserved. No part of this book may be used or reproduced in any manner whatsoever without written permission except in the case of brief quotations embodied in critical articles and reviews. For more information contact Roaming Lions Press at roaminglions@aol.com.

A Tear From A Glass Eye edited by Michele Golden & Dennis Zanabria. Cover Art by Julian Whitfield

ISBN 978-0-578-05551-0

First Roaming Lions Press Edition

For Donna, thanks for saving the dance.

Author's Introduction

    The following poems span a collective consciousness based on observations and a deep insight into the continual human condition and world around us. Stop, read and breathe. These poems should make you think. It is my hope that you, the reader, will not just read, but feel the words contained within this collection. If you do not feel, then I have not done right in my work.

    A majority of these poems were written during the bohemian phase of my life. I owe a debt of gratitude to all those who lent a couch and a smile to a wandering writer, especially Jen and Dirk. Thank you for letting me be me and for understanding who I am.

                                  Cheers!

                              John Golden
                              April 2, 2010

A Tear From A Glass Eye.

.

.

.

John Golden

Roaming Lions Press 2010

I
Epitaph Membership Card

time left swimming in circles

Clowns and Jugglers

An artist's ambition from the day you were born
Into a complex world of people and things
That could not
That would not
That would never understand you.
So full of life as a child
Even in your own
Private secluded world. Lost among
The abstractions and colors on a canvas.
Clowns, nurturing and forgiving with lucent
Eyes that hold the dreams and innocence of
A child.

Your eyes were entrancing, yet they
Also revealed a deep disturbance, a
Foreshadowing of things to come.
But for now things were alright,
You had the promise of a star,
Yet in the end, you would leave
Us all perplexed.
Never one for rules, You wanted to
Glance over the wall, had you only
Known the consequences it would bring.
Clowns, protective and nurturing, wanting
To hold you back, but you
Were never one to listen.

An orange, a plum and a matchbox. In these
Things lay your demise. 1966, a year
Full of interstellar voyages that
You would never return from.
Molded into a leader, though
Reluctant and unwilling,
But you were never one to listen,
Even to voices that came from inside.
Rock 'n' roll dreams that would
Foreclose on your future,

Leaving you a broken man
Standing among the frenzied masses.
Clowns, no longer among you,
Killed by the demons in your
Head that juggled your sanity
With uneasy hands.

Surrounded by hundreds, lost
Within a distant planet that
Existed out of madness.
Left alone to lament the mad
Indifferent to everything,
The wall had been broken.
Far from the clowns of your youth,
No longer Roger, no longer Syd,
Only a madcap hidden
Behind blank eyes.

Somewhere in time lies
A wall separating reality
From what is unknown.
Once you have crossed over
You can never return,
For reality has boundaries
That must lie unbroken.

It took you four short years
To scale the wall. The clowns
Are far gone and the jugglers
Stopped long ago. A dark
Cellar your dwelling, where
Your demons frolic among the shadows,
Yet still confined to your head.
The things that you must have seen,
Sentenced to insanity where worlds
Of regret dwell with the faded
Promises of a lost child who
Once believed in clowns.

Abstractions have painted your
Mind into a faded oblivion that
Floats between the folds of time.
Though still alive, you have
Never returned, living a life spawned
On rumors and false sightings.
A tragic cult hero not forgotten
But often gone.

Sometime ago I thought
I saw you while walking
Down a dim moonlit street.
A transparent illumination traveling
Among the shadows.
I called out for you…
Yet the madcap only laughed.

BARely Standing

Escalator floors catch
Me off guard as I
Stand up from the bar stool
I've been glued to for
The past four hours.

This bar is nothing more
Than a drive-in mortuary
With Christmas light coffin
Beer signs and barbarian
Bartenders expecting some
Sort of reward as they pass
Me the check and I sign
My will to death.

Epitaph for a Madman

Blood looks so appealing
In the moonlight
The sweet smell of death
Drifting up through the trees

Desperate screams carried
On the gentle breeze
As my starlit blade
Shines beneath the majestic sky
Reminding me that I am indeed a
God!

Epitaph for the Millennium

A cold chill fills the room.
Memories beckon
The faithful remain seated.
Death leads the ordinary
Into a doleful existence
Paving the path of the righteous
Into an oblivion of hell.

Shallow graves
Leave heavy spirits with
Magnetic crosses to bear
Retracting from all light
Drawn to the anguish and fear
That plague our fervent dreams.

I am left alone to watch
The insolence and aggravation
Starve us from our once
Promised salvation.
Spells are cast, but
The darkest charms break
Them all.

And we are left to dispose
Of our dignity.
A dusty horizon sprinkled
With hope, the mirage
Of the obsessed.

The cry of the insecure
Blossoming into wings that
Scorch the pale and solemn
Moonlight, which reveals
A shadow of us all.

Farewell to the Angels

Light can never shine as bright
As the angels. As bright as the
Light that shone from your eyes
The moment I first saw you.
As bright as a faint hope carried
By a distant dream. As bright as angels
Like you whose beauty shines a radiant
Light upon those they encounter.

I cannot hold what I do
Not have, for you were
Taken by another. Dreams
Could not mask the burden of
Reality, but your light shone
Bright throughout. Filling my
Eyes with colors and landscapes
Unlike anything I had ever seen.

Light that fills the darkness
Though only temporary, as if
To show for just a moment how
Beautiful life can be. Angels
Like you my dear from whom
The light is stolen
And it is you I'd like to thank
For briefly casting light upon
My soul.

Such beauty was not meant
To last, as it is true that
Angels fly and it is with this
Understanding that I have learned
To say goodbye.
Good luck in all you do my friend.
May God shine upon you with his grace
And though the world awaits you now
With open arms

Mine has become a darker place.

Growing Pains

The boulevard of regret is packed.
Its streets are lined with cars
And one cannot ignore the fact
That we all carry scars.

Existence equals sorrow
And this alone explains
Why we can't see a bright tomorrow
When our eyes are filled with pain
And as you lay yourself to sleep
Take comfort in this truth,
That wounds will never run as deep
As those we get in youth.

Home

This is where terror breeds
And fear resides, this is where
Heroes fall and faith crumbles.
Options are expired and time
Is nothing more than the
Reminder of a quiet desperation.
Solitude is as painful as
Company, for misery loves
Everyone.

This is where ravens' claws
Carve the memories of
fragmented dreams, flowers
Wither and pictures fade
Into an ocean of regret.
And all of the lost opportunities,
All the last chances, all of the
Screw ups come here to meet.
Come here to taunt and remind.
A shattered mirage beset by
Reality.

This is where children
Cry and freedom ends.
Happiness sets behind
The red glare of an unforgiving
Sun, this is where wings are
Clipped, innocence is lost and
Prayers dissolve with the dismal
Echoes of laughter.

This is where madness
Begins, where hope
Ends and death
Is as unwelcome as life.
For you cannot understand
Unless you've been here.

Your empathy is silenced by
Indifference, your advice
Is blackened by truth and
Your lies bring you
One step closer to us.
This…
Is where I live.

In Regards to Richard Cory

The things we think we want
Are often not the things we need
A vulgar wealth to flaunt
A compulsion fueled by greed

He walks the streets in style
And people know him well
But it's been quite awhile
Since he's seen the better side of hell

And those who begged for bread
Wish they had his place
But do not be misled
For he wears a painted face

And when the satin sheets
Lull him off to bed
He's left alone to greet
The demons in his head

A silver plated hell
Massive walls of pain
A lonely man who dwells
In the shadows of the sane

Many call him great
Admired for his wealth
That could not compensate
For his lack of mental health

Oh, when will we learn?
Did Richard die in vain?
All the money one could burn
Cannot pay off the creditors of pain

Inner City Lament

Seldom is faith captured
In a world such as ours.
For miracles cannot
Exist in a world full
Of swollen egos and
Arrogance. Beauty
Can never be discerned
Through eyes that
Only see in black and
White, and hate cannot
Survive unless it is accepted.

And so we turn our
Heads trying to ignore
The answer, all the while
Pretending a problem doesn't
Exist. Turning our backs on
Each other, on ourselves…
On life. Content to dwell in
A hollow world, never expecting
More out of ourselves than we
Do out of anybody else.

And still we stand permanently
Numbed, trying to restore our
Sanity. An eternal line waiting
To be followed. Straight ahead
In only one direction. And that is
Our future, that is all the wisdom life
Has to give to a race of creation
That refuses to look any
Further.

Jaded

I used to be stupid
Now I'm enlightened.
I used to be brave
Now I am frightened.

For I now realize
That ignorance is bliss.
Why did you have to open
My eyes to this?

Golden's Lament

People piss me off
With their little opinions
And self-righteousness.
Advice falls on deaf
Ears as my middle
Finger extends them
The kindest courtesy
I can offer.

Bailout Blues

Interior puzzlement, images
Of burning anarchy in
A Cadillac society full of
Tax form wristwatch alley cats
Who whirl around streets and
Buildings clutching the
New York Times, gathering
Euphoric kisses on Fifth Avenue.
Dead meat market policemen
Roam the streets with
Complicated hesitations
Turning their heads
To corporate crime
The new American passport.

Life

A constant velocity assures change
And a terrifying moment prolongs
Closure. The dark spaces are
Ours to fill as we please
Taking great consideration
To detail, painting as
A madman who relishes
A landscape, a lost freedom, a tempered
Moment lost forever among a crowd
Of fiends who fish for souls in
Sullen, dark, blackest night.

The highway is ours to follow
Though we did not pave it.
Only brief imprints left
Behind as we tirelessly
Tread through life.
A world where sin is not
An abomination, but a virtue
Carried by the disconsolate shadow of time.
Lost space is filled by the next
Wayward vagabond who clings to the
Last sliver of life he merits worth
Saving.

And all this boils down
To life.
Whether we embrace it
Or leave it,
We are all lured by its
Sordid promises, touched
By its maddening grip.
Burned by its raw honesty.
Like making love to
A memory, desperately
Hanging on to a tiny piece
Of nothing.

A faint blur
Smeared upon our souls.

Limerick

There was a three-legged dog named, "Drake"
Who liked sex with iguanas and snakes
Though his friends thought him vile
For screwing reptiles
They absolved him of all his mistakes.

Onslaught

They came from distant lands
Where dusty roads and injustice swallowed
Their dreams. Over giant hills of solitude,
Through barren fields where their fathers
Used to meditate. From straw huts loosely
Hinged together with mud, red like the
Blood that flowed through countless generations
Of suffering and hardships. From great
Majestic castles carefully carved out of stone
Leaving generations of history to mourn.
From beaches adorned in sunlight, where waves
Pounded at the shore. Where tides pulled
Their dreams far away into the endless abyss
Of night. They came because they knew
What it was like to die.

A faint buzz of hope carried through
The air, leading them out of their great
Castles, away from their gentle huts.
Away from their tranquil shores in search
Of a better life. What they did not know
Was that oppression knew no native
Land. Hate was not to be domesticated,
Prejudice was free flowing like the swollen
Rivers that swallowed their villages many years ago.

They came with tired eyes, with skeletons
That carried their dry cracked skin.
With an understanding of how cruel a
World could be. With infants on their
Backs and freedom on their tongues.
They came with injustice trailing only a footstep
Behind. They came because they knew what
It was like to die.

Tears for Twain

Newspaper graveyards blink
At the silence of the
Pigeons and whores who
Stumble through City Hall
Among the jockstrap pecking order
Where larks with dusty wisdom
Who call themselves leaders
Redefine a new America.
Tom Sawyer weeps from afar
Imagining the great
Mississippi River and its
Ancient freedoms and
Lessons on life.

Fortune cookie philosophers
Preaching in spiritual museums
Constipated ushers walk
Around shaking hands
With moldy ties and
Wooden gestures hanging on
Crowds listening to
Snobberies from carnival
Orators who preach about
A puzzling existence
Symbolic of a living question mark
While I hurry about searching
For a skiff to navigate
Through waters of grace
And imaginary scenes
Where Huck and Tom wait
Under an ecstatic moon
Looking for Jim in
The wounded wilderness
Of a lost American dream
Of eternal equality.

Timeless ideals washed

Away with the June rise
Entangled among the
Murky rocks and towheads
All the while men and women
Cast lines fishing for individuality
Assured rights born out of
"Old Glory" and patriotic madness
That once sold free towns
And empty prairies
Void of taxes and button-down
Senators hoisting up statues
Of masked paper loiterers
Holding parchments of circus
Tent truths that bleed
Out a promised liberty of what was
Supposed to be a free
And equal Shangri-la
Free of high theatrics
And slight-of-hand trickery

Salvation Fee

If misery loves company
Than I'm her greatest friend.
If anger is a way out
Than I have found an end.

Oppression yields passion.
Resistance gives way to bliss
And most are caught confused
Observing all of this.

And when the world
Stops turning, the desolate
Eye shall praise
A God that brings swift
Justice to a world set
In its ways.

Paradise cannot be found
When searching for its keys
For freedom does not harbor doors
Its entrance does come free.

The only admission accepted
Is the one etched on your soul
And if you've lived a life that's right
The key shall find the hole.

Sanity's Tomb

Empty feelings and broken mirrors
Where my future used to be.
Dreams and hopes now covered with dust.
The future, which was once put on hold
Now dwindles dimly before my eyes.
And as the blood runs from my nose,
Numbing my face, my desires.
Numbing my spirit, my dreams
        I am dying
        I am lost

I remember youth,
When nothing mattered, serenity ruled.
Happiness was found in all things,
Everything was new, everything was beautiful.
My soul was like a gift-wrapped box
Waiting to be opened on Christmas day.
I wanted to learn, to see, to feel.
The innocence of trust, the naiveté of hope,

But all that would soon fade
Fade into experience, into eyes that have seen
The hatred of the world.
Fade into a self-destruction that I could not control.
Now I remember…

That first line, first rush, intoxication
Freedom from reality, freedom from myself.
I remember the wind blowing lightly,
As a faint voice slipped into the dreary night,
The voices of a thousand who had gone
Before me, the voices of desperation and sorrow.
Their voices that echoed
        I am dying
        I am lost

But I would not listen, indulgence

Was my guide, freewill my enemy.
Enslaved to something much stronger
Than me.
Something I could not hold, nor feel or touch.
My life slowly being erased.
My existence snorted up my nose.
Years gone by in minutes,
Reality always right around the corner,
But I chose to escape into a snow-blind world
Where the arms of reason could
Not find me.

Outside of sanity's tomb
Lies the road to madness and excess
Where consequences are never spoken of,
Hedonism reigns and lives
Are ruined through self-indulgence.
Tomorrow never comes and the past is
But a faded whisper.
There's a fine line between happiness and desire
And if you choose the latter, you will surely pay the cost
A half spent life full of misery and regrets
        I am dying
        I am lost

Savior in Black (An Interior Monologue)

Interesting line of work I've chosen for myself.
But hey, I was always taught that it doesn't
Matter what you do, so long as you are happy.
Happiness, now there's a contradiction. It often seems
That the things that make us most happy are
The same things that bring us the most pain.
The things that eat away at our souls until
There's nothing left but the mere shadow
Of a man, the mere reflection of a shattered dream
That we once held for ourselves.

But hey, we all have our vices, neatly
Tucked away between the guilt and desires
That burn within us all. And I'm just a man
Caught in the middle trying to sell redemption
To those who know no other way. Besides
It's not really my job to care. I'm just a stepping
Stone toward the inevitable death that we
Must all someday face.

Oh, I suppose somewhere along the way I've
Been responsible for somebody's death, but haven't
We all? We've all killed parts of ourselves,
Parts of others, whether we realize it or not.
We all have blood on our hands, just as we have
Flesh and bone. We are all guilty in some
Small way. But guilt only represents the things that
We could never admit to ourselves, the little black
Secrets that we carry until our deaths. And I am
Exonerated from all this. For I know what I am.
I know what I do. I make no excuses for myself,
For I am aware of the consequences of my actions
And I am sure that someday I will burn in hell
For what I've done. The same hell that you are all
Trying to escape from.

I have seen men sell me their souls for what I

Have. Women sell off their dignity and self-respect like some
Gypsy at a swap meet. And for what? A temporary release
From the demons that will surely return the next day, just
As they have for God knows how long. What it all comes
Down to is control, a rare commodity in today's society.
I'm just an agent dealing time shares for the utopian world
We all dream of.

Perhaps I am evil, perhaps I have no morals. But
Morals are only good for setting boundaries, for putting
Up walls of guilt and shame that close us in, that strip us of our
vision
And freedom. Leaving us to pathetically wander like a
Lost herd of sheep. Ironically, I'm the model person for
I know not of race or gender. Old man
Or child, you're all the same to me. I have not the
Luxury of discrimination or conscience. And even those who
Oppose me, have come seeking refuge at one time or
Another. For every cross you have to bare, for every
Weight upon your shoulders, I have a shelf to put them on.
I can ease the pain. Behind my door lies your salvation.

Yes, I have come to terms with what I am. I am comfortable
In my own skin. But you are not, and that is why you
Need me. And when you come crawling I will be
There, giving my unconditional love for all you sick
Fucks. I cannot promise a better tomorrow, only an escape
From today. But soon tomorrow will become today
And I'll see you again, or perhaps I won't.
But you see, it is not my job to care.

9/11/01

Towers collapse revealing
The skeleton of our society
Freedom and security
On trial for all to see.
Fanatics render judgment
Sentencing us to a world
Of uncertainty.

Fire burns brightest
When controlled by one
Crippling all who
Dare to look into
Embers that glow
Revealing a history
All too often ignored

The oppressed become
Vigilantes and as God
Is great, so shall be
His justice, scales
Tipped in favor of a chosen
Few, the shell-shocked
Sit watching images
Of a crumbling world.
TV casualties of a new
World order.

There can be no God
Where there is war.
There is no justice
Where the blind lead.
Retaliation is swift
As God answers
The angry cry
Of America.

II
The Vagabond and the Couch

dry cleaning my coma clothes and picking up
lost inspirations on my way back home
to hang up my crooked shadow

4/15

Uncle Sam has his hand
Up my ass again.
Doesn't he know
I keep my wallet
On the nightstand?

A Silent Prayer

Soiled words, yellowing pages
Inspiration covered with dust.
Shall our muses become dead
Memories, left to wither on
A page of forgotten youth?

Untouched ideas are the world's
Greatest sin.
It's time to blow off the dust
Awaken ancient spirits and
Dance like crazed drunken fools.

Revolution through words, a great
Awakening of the collective conscious
Roaring down the streets like a possessed
Madman.

This is what I burn for, this is why I live.
The world can be great again, our hearts
Can be full
If only....
People would wake up.

A Collection of Half-Empty Glasses

Hangovers are like women,
They're terrible, yet
I keep coming back for more.

A Kind of Rebirth

Anxiety spreads its wings
Across the Western frontier
And television church altars.
Irradiated nationalism revival
Sweeps through discarded
American dreams while
I wait for the rebirth of
A safe world where
The artists and
Underground kings coexist
In unpremeditated harmony.
Heavenly circus men
Waltz like acrobats
Blind to decorated baboons
With collapsible morality
Who devour our fantastic future
Of sweet swaying truth.

Umbrage

Did you feel what I felt
While I held you within
My arms?
Did you feel the lies and deceit?
The need to feel accepted and loved?

Of course you did.
It's a drug we both need,
My lies create your smile.
My lust makes you feel pretty inside.
My soul is dying, just as you are
In my spider arms that inject
The promise of hope inside you.

The bastard and the blind
That is all we are.
Of course you didn't see.
I did
And unfortunately for you
I stopped feeling long ago.

Writer's Block (Everyone's Irish on St. Patrick's Day)

Words used to pour out of me
Long before the chaotic nights
Of drunken loneliness.
Searching for some kind of escape
Anything to stop the thoughts that swirl
Within my head.

Crazy behavior, strange laughter
Convincing me that anything was possible
While slowly taking my life.
Drowning in a sea of self-loathing,
Yet the words were always there,

Screaming to me, pleading for a release.
Lingering in the distance of a forgotten night
My soul was awakened.
Everyone's Irish on St. Patrick's Day.

I'm too old for this shit.
I want my words back.

Subtle Kind of Misery

Desolate whispers that echo down the
Hall of lost shadows, where I now dwell.
Waiting for something, yearning for the
Sort of promise that only tomorrow can bring.
Yet through it all, I patiently wait like
A dog anticipating the return of his long
Lost master.

I have wandered through the masses,
Walked among the crowds, only to go
Unnoticed, like the last shard of ice
That floats atop a half finished cocktail.
I have searched for inner peace,
Looked for a true love.
Only to be let down and misguided through
Life's charade of illusions and fallacies.

Though the years have been kind to me,
They have left my insides empty and rotting.
Like one who searches to recapture the innocence
Of lost youth, only to be scorched by
The unforgiving hands of time.

And through it all I have endured
Lead by the faint light of hope
That burns within us all.

I have looked towards the sky many times
And asked for answers, like a sailor
Lost at sea who prays to some foreign god.

Time after time redemption has
Eluded me, never to be found within
The mortal boundaries of men.
The type of penance that the bum
Finds in his bottle, that
The mother finds in the eyes of her children.

True happiness and peace are a sublime
Ignorance that lie within the eyes
Of a child.
A cunning and fallacious
Assassin that weaves its way
In and out of our lives,
Leaving only the stench of reality
Hanging in the stagnant air.

I do not wish to be perfect,
Only happy. To separate myself
From the evil selfish ways of
Man. To surge through the lies
And scandal that plagues us
Like the sort of freedom only a condemned man
Can appreciate. To want,
To let go of life, to shutter, to flee.
When every breath taken
Brings a subtle kind of misery.

Say Goodbye to Kansas

The chalice calls and so
You shall dance, enslaved
To the nectar of folly
Every sip mocks you as
You try to carve out an existence
In what you so pathetically call
A life

Hot liquid poison runs through your
Veins, drowning out your vision
And self-respect. Immoral intentions
Strewn over the yellow bricks
Paving a road of self-destruction.
At the end stands your truth, behind
A shrewd curtain constructed of severed
Promises and forgotten dreams.
The wizard is indeed a fool
As are all those who seek
The selfish vices found within
Themselves.

So click your heels together
Young man and understand that
There is no hell quite like the
One you make when you live for
Every superficial self-indulgence that
Your solemn spirit yearns for. The
Future is set ablaze as cloven
Hooves and pointed fingers
Await your arrival.
Oh when will you learn
That every vice you entertain
Stokes the fire that
Will one day consume
Your very soul

Shadow Stalker

Sometimes it gets better
And I forget that I
Hurt. Memories
Haunt me like ghosts
Gathering on a highway.
Transparent hallucinations
Against black asphalt
And I retreat further into
A frozen isolation
Pierced by shards of
Time gone by.

Moonlight cures a
Poisoned mind though
Within hours sunlight
Will cause an almost
Certain relapse.
God bless the
Creatures of the night.

Scotch on the Rocks

Kick starts my day
Blurring the kaleidoscope
Possibilities and thin line reality.
I need this medicine to
Silence my unsettled conscience

Occupies my lunch hour
Eroding my tension
With its sweet waves
Of comfort, making
The hell I must return
To a little more
Tolerable

Lulls me to sleep
With its sordid lies
Assuring a better tomorrow
With every swallow.

Insomnia

I'm not shining anymore.
I feel a bit burnt out.
Wallowing through the
Depths of night
Feeling fear and doubt.
Is there any world
Out there at all?

Thoughts on Graduation Day

Between life and death
I'll choose a happy medium
Upon which to write my
Epitaph. Lost souls in
The nine to five graveyard searching
For a purpose as they eek out
A living, constantly looking
For their discarded humanity.

There is no knowledge to
Be found in the masses
Only followers content
To have others choose their
Happiness.
There can be no
Shining light in the sphere
Of conformity, only silent
Hopes to be trampled by
The feet of millions.

This is the contemptible reality
That so many miscall their
Lives. I will not go, I
Refuse to follow. Obscurity
Paints defiant wings
And I shall fly away on
No wing but mine.

Evening Creeps

Incognito no more
Too much revealed
On a simple drunken
Night of starlit
Dust and visions
Of a new you
Awakened in a state
You once abandoned

Your charm magnified
Through a rekindled passion
And sleepy bar
Shadows creeping along
A dark velvet floor
Where I follow your
Eyes looking for
An acknowledgment that
I am not alone
In seeing your beauty

502 (Knockout Punch)

Bloodshot eyes
Shoot the pavement
A final glance.

Claro's '92

Old toothless man
Reeking thick of whiskey and urine
Going to wager
His meager fortunes
At the racetrack.

Modern Day Prophet

The streetwalker is
Wise.
She knows where she's
Going.
Do you?

Awful Truth

I was baptized by a priest
Who got caught with
An underage male prostitute and
Some chickens
And you have the nerve
To ask me why I sin.

Starving Siddhartha

Wounded Buddha glancing
At life's dying memory.
Trapped symbols among
Hallucinatory mountains caught
In the charcoal fog
Where falcons dive into
Threaded graves of
Imagined battlements of
Nirvana seekers led astray.

Invasion of Privacy

Bleach blonde Barbie
Sporting a tramp stamp tattoo
Why do you soil
My paradise?

Summoned for a Guest Appearance

There is a difference between
Nirvana and sobriety.
One you attain through knowledge
The other you get
Through a court order.

Observations at The Garden of Eden Junkyard

Orange tree
How I see your
Rotting children
On the ground.

The Vegetarian and the Cannibal

It's cold outside
And I have deceived you
With my pitchfork tongue
And sincere eyes.
You cry out for me
And I do not answer.

I only wanted a moment
And you expected eternity.
Perhaps I am a bastard
But you trust too easily.

How the heart can be
Fooled with just a few
Words.
Why do I matter to you?
Don't you know I'm just like
The others who filled
You with hope
Only to suck your precious
Life's blood away.

We're all pecking vultures
Clawing at crushed red
Velveteen dresses, pulling
At long rose stem fingers
Just to hear you utter
Those fatal three
Words.

Washing away your trust
And innocence. Basking
In your tears while our
Guilt flies through the window
Into the sordid night.

I found you.

I made you.
I blew you up only to deflate
You like a child's birthday balloon.
I am a pig.
I am all that is wrong.
I am every bit human.
I am mankind.
I am legion
And you are nothing more
Than a stain on my conscience.

Common Sense

I just voted for Ozzy.
That's right, Ozzy Osbourne.
Hell, he makes as
Much sense as anyone
Else.
Aren't all politicians
Loony bastards?

Resurrection Delayed

Easter morning
Parents hiding brightly colored
Eggs for sleepy-eyed children
As I smoke on my porch
Contemplating the
State of America.

We can all shine as brightly
As those neon eggs
If we could only
Come out of hiding
And yell to the cloudless
Sky, "I am alive!
I am a living, thinking
Member of a free society!"

But good intentions
Hide behind the sad
Truth that as
Soon as I extinguish
My cigarette, I'll
Go back inside and
Watch TV.

Coffeehouse Blues

Her eyes bleed lust
Confusing my fragile thoughts
Like a lost river in a wilderness
Of doubt
Flowing toward an uncertain end
That surely even God must laugh at.

III
Graveyard Gypsies

hollow graves, open for spitting

Vacation

I sleep until six in the evening
The daylight is much
Too formal
For a wretch like me.
Who will drown
The daylight that
Makes monsters
Of us all?

Withered Rose

Love is danger
Sweet chaos
Torn from our souls
Always handed back.

Neon Playground

Simple things annoy me.
There is beauty in chaos.
Such is the
American night.

Ozone Conspirator

The paper burns slow,
Smoke inhaled as the Marlboro
Man gives his last parting gasp
And I stand among the millions
Of hopeless addicted fools, clutching
On to a fragment of peace five minutes
At a time.
We all pay for our funerals in the end.

Smokey's Curse

Logs fall in the serene Sierra Nevada landscape.
Who wants to hear the lumberjack's song?
Not I, not mother nature, only the corporate
Suits who turn the precious pulp
Into blood money that sends us
Scurrying like rats among the
Ivory pillars created by lust.

Goddamn Uncle Sam, I wish
I was adopted.
Red, white and screwed
And singing the blues
Of a nation's forgotten
Freedom.

If only I had a saw.
There are a few things
That I would like to cut down.

Ugly Truth

I wish my heart
Was big enough
To give to everyone
Selfish whims consume me.

Surrendered Aggression

Night comes down bringing
Its sweet songs, a temporary release
From the monotonous drone of the day.
Darkness can hide what the daylight
Is so cruel to reveal.

Starlight has the power to heal
The deep-set scars that
This world can cast across
Our face. The hazy smoke
Of midnight's intoxication
Leaves me spellbound standing
In rapture, on the edge of
A blurred epiphany.

"I love you," she whispered
As she silently slipped into
The night, leaving me with the
Torn images of a dream
I once held. Haunted lullabies
Soothe lost children and
Neon mirages lure the vice
Ridden disciples of Los Angeles
Into another night of paradise.

Yet those who really know
Choose to stay in. Why
Travel when misery makes
House calls for free? My fingers
Throb, bleeding from playing the
Cruel chords of life. My heart silently
Heads out on the next passing storm
Venturing to bring back some sort
Of answer to me. Chasing the
Phantom dragon of peace that
Taunts us all.

The keys to the kingdom no
Longer work, for the locks
Have been changed, leaving
Me alone like a dog in
The rain. "I love you" are
Words that should never be
Spoken. Expectations so high
Can never be met, only crumble
Like an ancient city swept
Away in a flood. Swollen
Rivers eat villages and heartless
Women swallow men like
Aspirin on a Sunday morning.

My mind is held captive
By insecurity and fear.
Craving the asylum that
The condemned man
Prays for and the madman
Runs from. Giant
Walls of insanity built
On foundations of guilt,
So deep-rooted that not
Even a thousand years of
Erosion could move them.

Passion is a fire that glows
And all fires must eventually
Die. It is up to us to
Restart what has refused
To burn. Embers carry away
Dreams with their soft
Glow, drifting into the
Endless folds of the night,
And it is there where I now dwell.

As midnight's child I
Burn with a nocturnal
Desire that has taught

Me to hate the light.
To hide from what is
Seen, cursed to roam
Among the shadows
Held captive by
Their secrets and enamored
With their sorcery.

Crooked politicians hide behind
Adamantine doors with harlots
Appointed to their highest courts.
Jesters mock the righteous with
Temptation and clowns scare
The children with images of
What their future holds. The earth
Spins infinitely, desperately
Trying to escape what it
Can no longer hold, and
God sits from afar and
Watches wondering if
We're even worth
Saving anymore.

Books cannot teach what
History refuses to remember.
Knowledge can shed light on
A bliss so bright that
The sane could never
Dare to look into it. And still
I search, looking for a perfect
Truth, looking for a hole
In the darkness to escape
From.

Words are the only things
That can fill this void.
Poetry, the only remedy
For a broken heart
And tortured soul. And

So I keep writing until
The void is filled. Until
I understand, until I can
No longer feel the sorrows
Of this world.

The Small Hours of Countless Days

I walk down the cracked streets
That used to be home to much
Happier days, past the old
Schoolyard where I used to play,
Content in the endless days that define
Youth. Watching the herds of children
Who playfully frolic, shrugging
All responsibilities, lost within
The confines of kickball or tag, living
In the very moment. No concerns
Of the past or worries of tomorrow.
And as I watch them, I'm reminded
Of a much simpler time.
And for a moment I am lost.
The burdens of the world are lifted.
        And I only do this
        Because it works.

Five o'clock, the bell chimes
As I punch my card and rise from
The fog of the blue collar world
That I am now enslaved to.
Acres of cars fill the streets
With thousands who head home
Trying to make sense of it all.
Knowing there's nothing left to
Look forward to but another day
Of having the life sucked out of them.
And as the highway becomes an ocean
Of metal and dim lights, I pray
For the strength to make it through
Another day.
        And I only do this
        Because it works.

Opening the door, I am greeted
By an unsympathetic wife

Who I no longer hold love
For. All that is left now
Is a sick sort of contentment
That I carry for her.
The deep burning passion that I
Once felt for her has dried up
Like the last piece of fruit
That hangs from a rotting tree.

I make my way past the dull
Hum of the TV, into the kitchen
And open the door to my makeshift
Altar. I pull out the dark
Green bottle and retreat to the couch,
Counting down the hours until I pass out.
The only true escape I have
Anymore. My wife glares
At me from across the room
With accusing eyes, wondering
Why the hell I do this to myself,
Watching me slowly drink my life away.
                                    And I only do this
                                    Because it works.

Musings on My Future Wife

If only she knew the way
Her mere presence lights up
A room.
If she only knew
The way my heart stops
At the mere mention of
Her name.
Beauty such as hers
Is more than a gift, it is a miracle.
A solace only to be
Found on the wings
Of eagles.
A voice only to be heard
In the laughter of children.
A dream that lights a passion
Carried away on roaming clouds
Into the tranquil night.

                    Yet there is pain and angels
                    Weep, for she notices
                    None of this.

And every time I
Hold her, I'm reminded
Of heaven. Every time
I hold her I understand
Why eagles fly, why
Stars shine and why
The sun sets. For
Eagles fly high
Above on tired
Wings searching
For a paradise that
Must exist somewhere.
The sun sets on a world
That is far too self-absorbed
To notice the
Awe-inducing beauty

It shines, and children
Laugh because only
They can see past all
The heartache and pain. They
See the beauty that is
All around.
The beauty that I see in her.

                                        And she notices none of this
                                        And this is why I cry.

Truth

Heroes tread where freedom
Ends and angels fly wherever
They please
And though the world
Is born again, it is
Never free of disease.

Twilight's Blanket

The sun shines bright to open sleeping eyes.
Another night has slowly disappeared
Somewhere into the distant folds of time.
She rises up to greet the new found day
Aware that somehow things have stayed the same.
The mirror stares back hard to contemplate
The lonely eyes that stare into its face.

The child cries out from somewhere down the hall,
A piercing echo of reality.
Reminding her that things have got to change,
Reminding her that he has gone away.
And though there's many travesties in life
The single mother shines above them all.

The cold winds of the fall against her lips
Remind her that another year has passed,
Remind her that he's never coming back.
And still two jobs are not enough to feed
The shining eyes that stare up from below.
And though she tries so hard to get ahead
She always seems to be a month behind.

The sun sets low to end another day,
The soft glow of the moon carries her pain.
The bright eyes from below look up with love
And somehow she knows that it's all ok.
And even though he's never coming back,
And even though her worries weigh a ton.
She has the strength to fight another day,
She gets it from the love found in her son.

The starlight shimmers gently through the trees,
Sweet lullabies that echo down the hall.
A certain peace which few can understand
Sustained within the arms of a mother.
A distant owl somewhere lulls her to sleep,

Her child fast asleep within a dream.
The warm lights of heaven's welcoming call,
And though there's many beauties found in life
The single mother shines above them all.

Zen

Empty is the soul who
Does what he is told.
Happy is the man who
Makes his own freedom.
And then there is me
Standing in the middle
Simply content to exist.

Corporate Suits and Leather Boots

Ass kissing, self-absorbed
Full of good intentions.
Cold, shallow and
Obscene.
A picture perfect invention.
How everyone must
Aspire to be as grand
As you.
Programmed hollow soldiers
Who do not have a clue.

You're so quick to follow
Rules and please the
Status quo.
People are only
Numbers...
To you.

Perspective on the Night

Night's darkest landscapes
Hold a myriad of color
Seen through the discourse of time.
Lost angels and nymphs drift
Through the hazy starlight
Sublime travelers who
Hold a consciousness far too
Beautiful for the world
To contain.

Roll Me One Kenobi and The Red Eye Knights

Original hipsters would
Have dreaded the day
When any douchebag
With a fro hawk and a card
Could seek enlightenment.

It used to be about adventure
In the wild American night
Roaming through alleys
And shady apartments.
It used to be about
A community of free thinkers
Ready for revolution and intellectual
Revolt.

Underage kids with
Fake IDs following
A bureaucratic endorsed
Trend.
Nobody sings of freedom anymore.

Another legal high, like two dollar
Wine cheapened by a generation
Of trend following conformists.
$150 dollars and you've got
A corporate membership card
To another government program.

So sit back at your little
Party and know that the
Same government who
Has had its spoon in
Your mouth for all
Of these years is now
Infiltrating your lungs.

Keep convincing yourself

That you're a rebel, a freedom
Fighter, while you pack one
With your Abercrombie &
Fitch shirt and press ironed
Hair with your arm band tattoo
And two hundred dollar shades.
Without an original thought
Swirling through your gel
Styled head.

What happened to being
Original?
What happened to the artists
And the poets?
The ones who thought
Deeply and loved with
A burning passion brighter
Than any neon slogan or
Stamp on a government card.

Multicolored Optimism

Part I: The Trip

    Lemonade landscapes,
    Hazy green eyes.
    Infinite escape,
    Float through the sky.

    Nocturnal dwelling
    From the land far below
    Happiness selling
    For those in the know.

    Silver light shining
    Rainbows in trees
    Abstraction mining
    And memory fees.

    Mist from the ocean
    Shadows in tides
    Earth spinning in motion
    Along for the ride

    Colors that trail
    Eyes that deceive
    Life's never stale
    When on LSD

Part II: Reality Gone/Insanity Creeps

    Tie-dyed dimensions
    In the folds of your mind
    Ambitions and intentions
    Too far gone to find

    Realms of the insane
    That lie on your tongue
    Shelves in your brain

Where sanity is hung

Boundaries are broken
Time is just a word
Consequences spoken
Too often unheard

A lifetime of answers
A look from within
Ironclad dancers
That repent for your sins

The more that you take
The sooner you'll find
The hell that you make
When trapped in your mind

For Edna*

Deep reflections reveal a sullen past,
And the sun's bright rays paint an
Uneven picture where a familiar face
Used to dwell, content in the light of being.
Oh, but Edna, you were never one
To be tied down by the burdens of life.

A moonlit summer night, wrapped within
The seductive arms of the ocean.
A divine epiphany that renews
A spark of life, yet unveils a quiet discontent.
The earth and all creation for one moment
Stood in divine beauty and harmony,
The bewitching hour close at hand
While ancient spirits encompassed a starlit sky.

A thousand emotions ran through you
Bringing you to a sudden awakening
So subtle, yet it could not be ignored.
Your former self faded like an old pair
Of blue jeans, lost among the silver oaks
The night left a deep cicatrix across your soul,
You would never be the same again.

To know one's self is never easy
Dreams and desires were meant to be chased,
Aspirations were meant to be guarded like gold.
The unessential could be shed,
But never again would you sacrifice
Your being....your soul....yourself.

You felt so much and your passions
Shone off of you casting a beautiful
Halo of love and freedom.
Your eyes raged with life and carried a gentle
Light which revealed the poetry of a tortured mind.
Your courage brought strength to me,

Your every thought studied like a fine piece of art.

Wisdom brings sweet pain and knowledge
Carries a heavy tax that can never be paid.
Your art could only bring temporary
Peace, and gentle music carried you away
Into a shallow garden where you
Were too susceptible to the sorrows of the world.
Love held no guarantees and life
Was too unstable to rely on.

Your torment, an empty vessel set afloat
On a sea of discord and doubt.
Your mind contaminated by "le mal du siècle"*
Your soul thrown into melancholy exile,

And as you took your final descent
Into the enchanted waters of the gulf
The ocean once again embraced you,
And its still waters cleansed you of your life.
How the angels must have wept with grief,
How every creature must have hung their head
In quiet desperation, lamenting a life so new.
And though the wind may spread your ashes
And the ocean may erode your body,
Your memory will live on
Just like the dreams you once chased.

* Edna: Edna Pontellier, the main character in Kate Chopin's novel <u>The Awakening</u>
* Le mal du siècle: French for "the sickness of the century"

It's the Little Things That Lead to Divorce

Dark night
Lying in bed
Screams echo down the hall.
She lies still, half naked and bruised.
Dogs hate baths.

All I See is Stars

Newton's laws of gravity
Title forces (different gravitational force)
Newton's modification of Kepler's 3rd law
Doppler effect (red shift, blue shift)
Stefan-Boltzmann law
Intensity of radiation varies with distance
What is the net reaction of a proton chain?
Factors that determine escape velocity
Expansion of the universe
Closure of the universe (or will it keep expanding?)
Hertzsprung-Russell Diagram
Schrödinger's cat
Where do red and white dwarfs
Lie on the Hertzsprung-Russell diagram?
How long is the sun expected to remain a
Main sequence star?

When I look into the autumn sky
All I see is stars.
I sometimes feel like
Schrödinger's cat in that
Baleful, deadly box.
A perfect analogy
For the world and
The existence that
God has meticulously
Carved out for us.
Quantum mechanics
Perfectly describing
The human state.
Superposition of states
We are all half-dead
And half-alive.
When will the stars
Reveal their secrets?

Haiku #1

She wears a false smile
That nobody can see through
Her pain stays muted

Haiku #2

Shallow rock river
Drunkenly drifting along
Past pine tree shadows

Haiku #3

Solid red lights that
Prolong my misery as
I make my way home

Haiku #4

Somber black ocean
You make pirates out of the
Poets and junkies

Haiku #5

Five is not a lot.
Seven is a bit better
But still not enough

Haiku #6

Paris forgive me
I am not worthy of your
Beautiful landscapes

Haiku #7

Six A.M. sunrise
Reminding me that I still
Haven't stopped writing

Haiku #8

Red leather bar chairs
Cracked mahogany tables
Serving up cheap beer

Haiku #9

I stepped in dog shit
On the way to check the mail
Forgot it's tax day

Haiku #10

Her black painted nails
Lure me into ecstasy
Where lonely men dwell

Haiku #11

Watching the news is
Like a cheap five minute high
That scratches our souls

Haiku #12

One could do much worse
Than writing for a living
Not that I would know

Haiku #13

Majestic redwood
Reminding me that I'm far
Away from Japan

Haiku #14

Vagrant alley cat
Steps on to the warm sidewalk
Casting a quick glance

Haiku #15

Wind hits the palm fronds
The shutter door creaks and shakes
A gentle spring storm

Haiku #16

Green German bottle
Imported from St. Louis
Eroding my thoughts

Haiku #17

Dirty hands soil
Her pristine ironing job
On the hotel floor

Haiku #18

I'm burning again.
Typewriter junkie lost in
A sweet sea of words

Haiku #19

Frosted hair phony
Bad makeup and a guitar
Where's my music gone?

Haiku #20

Smog stained skyscrapers
Vision of Los Angeles
Not my paradise

IV
Nocturnal Nomads

Last breath used for ordering Chinese take out

Starstruck Superman

Souls are like kryptonite
Oozing plastic insincerity
Salvation through the
Camera's eye as
We vicariously live
Through the stripped
Dignity of others

Self-help doctors
Claiming to save
Those in need
While shamelessly
Exploiting them
Everybody wants their
Fifteen minutes of fame

The sick and dying
Pining for the cameraman
Dancing to the alluring
Sound of the death rattle
When did fame become
More important than humanity?

Your crocodile tears supercede your
Ego driven ambition
You're as sick as
Those you claim to help
You self-righteous pricks

Your pompous authority precedes
Your ostentatious smile
To you ratings equal
Deliverance, a Nielsen approved
Cure for damaged goods
You crush like aluminum
Cans to be recycled
For another episode

So put on your suit
And save the world
You arrogant bastards
Celebrity gets priority
In this waiting room
No need for insurance cards
You've already paid a hefty
Price with your integrity

Fly high above buildings
And cities with your
Inflated egos and
False sense of importance
Forgetting that people do
Indeed hurt and that
We all have fragile
Stained glass souls
That shatter with
Every publicly televised
Humiliation, breakdown and fight
That you so eagerly anticipate

You better grab your capes
You selfish fucks
You're gonna need 'em

I Only Have Ides for You

Caesar did not heed the warning.
Most women don't either
Or anyone else
For that matter

No hand is more cruel
Than that of a
False friend hiding
Behind jealousy and
A hidden agenda.

Changing of the Guard

If our cocks were
The size of our egos
We would truly be monsters

Waiting for the Cuckoo to Fly Again

Silver machine wheels
Of society that constantly
Turn with a thunderous roar
Droning out any semblance of reason

I can hear the machinery
Subconsciously aware that
I've been programmed on
A path since birth

Who will pull us out of the fog?
There are no more Lennon's
Or McMurphy's to breathe
Reason into a collective insanity

Starched nurse brings
Me my meds, but she
Forgot to leave the room key
Chief went AWOL decades ago

Even Kesey flew the nest
A few years back
Leaving behind a bus
And the message that
I missed the last train
Out of societal enslavement

Reunion of Sorts

There's sarcasm
In her eyes that
Masks the pain
Among strangers in a bar
And a long lost friend.

LAX (Friday Night)

Voltaic blue towers
Leading me into a
Sphere of chaos. The
Excited and the impatient meet.
Some for adventure,
Some with remorse.
All drifting, swimming
In a tide of circular anarchy
Palm trees stir in
The electric breeze.
Welcome to Los Angeles.
LAX doesn't seem so bad
After a couple of Xanax
And a six-pack.

Somewhat Considerate

Didn't mean to dig a hole
For both of us to
Get stuck in.

I've made it out
On my own
Now I just need
To find a shovel
To throw down
To you so you
Can make your own path.

Generation 2000

The dying art of letters
Starving for a stamp
And a thought.
Texting to eradicate
Sins and bad grammar
As the postman cries
In the harsh afternoon
Sunlight.

Return of the Nomad

I live in a paradise
That I far too seldom
Visit.

The ripples in the water
Beckon me saying
"Where have you been?"
The wind drifts through
The palm trees welcoming
My return.

Tranquil boats and runners
Cast shadows in the sunset
As I try to explain
My absence to a busy
Ocean that cannot
Grasp the idea that
I have been bogged
Down with work.

And still the currents beat
Against the old sea wall
Full of tales about
People like me
Who just can't seem
To understand that
Nature has no time card.

The Shadow of Mr. Myers

Gas lamp ghosts
Dancing in the fog.
How the smell of autumn
Awakens us all
On a drunk wandering
Suburban night.

Bear Market Blues

Talk is cheap
Hookers aren't.
Taxes are expensive too.
Come to think of it
My accountant is
A bit of a prostitute.
We're all just whores
Turning tricks for Uncle Sam.

The Memories of Ghosts

Long lost love and
Stale reflections swirling
In violence like a
Noisy subway train at night
                              Only the broken hearted
                              Contemplate life

Stolen champagne memories
Her eyes as thick as boards
Scornful wretched night
What have you left us
When the weak have
Nothing but faded
Afflictions to
Keep the time by
                              Only the broken hearted
                              Contemplate life

Sweet velvet singer
Throw your haunting voice
Around me and take
Me back to better days
For the trains are
Getting much too loud
                              Only the broken hearted
                              Contemplate life

Dusty picture frames
Cleaned by tears
Shaking hands hold
Empty treasure chests
That turn to sand
And disappear
                              Only the broken hearted
                              Contemplate life

Another Lost Evening

Shards of etched glass
Hit the floor
Another marriage
Dissolved by the
Crimson hands of alcohol.

It's All Who Ya Know

I got a letter from the
Devil's son-in-law.
Seems he won't be taking over
His brother-in-law got
The gig.
He's a bit pissed off,
After all he's the one
With the Ph.D., the
Well-rounded man of learning

His brother-in-law
Is a military brat with
Just a stamp and a suitcase
Playing his guitar in
Midnight's lonely graveyards.
A lazy bum just sittin'
At the crossroads
With an out of tune guitar
And the faint smell of
Brandy on his breath

The letter paints a picture
Of bitterness and envy
Etched on a fretboard
Of genius.
Just another unemployed
Bastard with connections
And bad intentions.

Lost in Central California

Cheap dime store whore
Take me away in
Your rusted two-cylinder
Chariot
To the dusty planes
Of Bakersfield
Where every cowboy
Rides a tractor
And wears a mesh hat.

Don't Talk to Strangers

Left my watch on a park bench.
Some asshole came running up to
Me to return it.
Why does everyone have
To keep a schedule?

Winston and the Prole

Cracked lips on an
Old woman make
Sinners of us all.

Observations From a Honda

Darts fly by leaving trails of light.
Weary travelers glued to a dashboard
Time clock.
Yellow light posts to keep
Out the fog.

I could use one of those
To free me from the prison
Of my unstable mind.

Sunscream

A spot upon my skin
Left over from the sun
And all the beaches where I've been
Cancer is not much fun.

Coming to Grips

My child isn't Mozart.
I caught him stuffing
Blocks up his nose.
He's thirteen for fuck's sake

Waiting Room Junkie

Patience is not a virtue.
It's a pain in the ass.
When you're sitting
In a disease ridden
Chair waiting for
Your name to be called
As five o'clock traffic
Piles up on the death
Trap we call a freeway.

Shaking and sweating
Growing angrier by
The dull empty minute.
Just give me my
Fucking pills and
I'll be on my way.

Coughing children frolic
Among the green chairs.
Sales reps jump ahead of me
Along with everyone else
Leaving me stranded
And alone among
The germ-strewn magazines.
This is horseshit.
I have an appointment.

Stone-faced receptionist
Darts accusing stares my
Way.
She knows that
I'm just here for a fix.
Nothing wrong with me
Just another addict
Waiting for a prescription.

Dishonor Roll

To all of you soccer moms
With your pristine vans
And student of the month
Bumper stickers of bravado
Do you know that your
Kids have smoked more
Dope and had more sex
In your suburban dream machines
Than you could ever imagine...
Have fun at practice

Wrong Address

I didn't mean to interrupt
Your pity party with my logic
And thoughts
But your invitation didn't say
What to bring
I'll leave my gifts on the table
And politely show myself to the door

The Lost Years (Vol.1)

Pool shark death hall
I cup my mouth on the
Way to the bathroom where
I vomit out the night's blind ambitions
My songs are playing on the jukebox
The ice is melting in my whiskey
And my conscience is rotting among
Savages and another misspent weekend

Big Red Stolen Savior

West Park School District
Stolen words that I
Need to fill up this
Notebook journal mind
Of mine

Uneasy flame too close
To the curtains will
Only rest when I've
Burnt through the
Night and the secluded
Forests of thought
That grow in the
Gentle moonlight,
A fine substitution for
Solace found in nature

Ghost pen prophet gunslinger
Shooting words into the
Depths of darkness
Hunting for stars
To bring back to
My solitary apartment

A balcony of collective
Imbalance that teeters
With every drop of
Ink poured onto paper
This...
Is how I write

John Golden is a writer and a hopeless Rock 'n' Roll addict who currently resides in Long Beach, CA. He has been writing since kindergarten when he used to dictate poems to his mother. When he's not writing or teaching he can be found contemplating the moon and all things nocturnal.

John Golden's debut book of poetry, ***A Tear From A Glass Eye*** was recently released. John also took part in contributing poetry in the Roaming Lions Press sampler, ***Sons of the Silent Age*** (2010).

Photograph by Dennis Zanabria
Long Beach, California

CONTENTS, COMETS, CONQUESTS.

I. Epitaph Membership Card
Clowns and Jugglers 13
BARely Standing 16
Epitaph for a Madman 17
Epitaph for the Millennium 18
Farewell to the Angels 19
Growing Pains 21
Home 22
In Regards to Richard Cory 24
Inner City Lament 25
Jaded 26
Golden's Lament 27
Bailout Blues 28
Life 29
Limerick 31
Onslaught 32
Tears for Twain 33
Salvation Fee 35
Sanity's Tomb 36
Savior in Black (An Interior Monologue) 38
9/11/01 40

II. The Vagabond and the Couch
4/15 43
A Silent Prayer 44
A Collection of Half-Empty Glasses 45
A Kind of Rebirth 46
Umbrage 47
Writer's Block (Everyone's Irish on St. Patrick's Day) 48
Subtle Kind of Misery 49
Say Goodbye to Kansas 51
Shadow Stalker 52
Scotch on the Rocks 53
Insomnia 54
Thoughts on Graduation Day 55
Evening Creeps 56
502 (Knockout Punch) 57
Claro's '92 58
Modern Day Prophet 59

Awful Truth 60
Starving Siddhartha 61
Invasion of Privacy 62
Summoned for a Guest Appearance 63
Observations at The Garden of Eden Junkyard 64
The Vegetarian and the Cannibal 65
Common Sense 67
Resurrection Delayed 68
Coffeehouse Blues 69

III. Graveyard Gypsies
Vacation 73
Withered Rose 74
Neon Playground 75
Ozone Conspirator 76
Smokey's Curse 77
Ugly Truth 78
Surrendered Aggression 79
The Small Hours of Countless Days 83
Musings on My Future Wife 85
Truth 87
Twilight's Blanket 88
Zen 90
Corporate Suits and Leather Boots 91
Perspective on the Night 92
Roll Me One Kenobi and The Red Eye Knights 93
Multicolored Optimism 95
For Edna 97
It's the Little Things That Lead to Divorce 99
All I See is Stars 100
Haiku #1 101
Haiku #2 101
Haiku #3 101
Haiku #4 102
Haiku #5 102
Haiku #6 102
Haiku #7 103
Haiku #8 103
Haiku #9 103
Haiku #10 104
Haiku #11 104
Haiku #12 104

Haiku #13 105
Haiku #14 105
Haiku #15 105
Haiku #16 106
Haiku #17 106
Haiku #18 106
Haiku #19 107
Haiku #20 107

IV. Nocturnal Nomads
Starstruck Superman 111
I Only Have Ides for You 113
Changing of the Guard 114
Waiting for the Cuckoo to Fly Again 115
Reunion of Sorts 116
LAX (Friday Night) 117
Somewhat Considerate 118
Generation 2000 119
Return of the Nomad 120
The Shadow of Mr. Myers 121
Bear Market Blues 122
The Memories of Ghosts 123
Another Lost Evening 124
It's All Who Ya Know 125
Lost in Central California 126
Don't Talk to Strangers 127
Winston and the Prole 128
Observations from a Honda 129
Sunscream 130
Coming to Grips 131
Waiting Room Junkie 132
Dishonor Roll 133
Wrong Address 134
The Lost Years (Vol.1) 135
Big Red Stolen Savior 136

www.ingramcontent.com/pod-product-compliance
Lightning Source LLC
Chambersburg PA
CBHW030046100426
42734CB00036B/374